PhotoSecrets

YOSEMITE

The Best Sights and How To Photograph Them

"Today, after 35 mountain expeditions to such places as the Himalaya, Alaska, and Patagonia, I am able to return to Yosemite and to say with the authority of extensive personal experience how truly unique the park is. I have found nothing like it in the rest of the world, no place where so many virtues of beauty, fine weather, ease of cross-country travel, biological diversity, and wilderness come together to form such a complete mountain paradise."

From *Galen Rowell's Vision: The Art of Adventure Photography.*

Foreword

By Galen Rowell

By Greg Heisler for Mountain Light

Galen Rowell is an internationally renowned wilderness photographer and author. His writings and photographs appear in *Life*, *National Geographic*, *Sports Illustrated*, and *Outdoor Photographer*.

Galen was scaling Sierra peaks by the age of ten, and had made over 100 first ascents by thirty. In 1984 he received the Ansel Adams Award for his contributions to the art of wilderness photography. Galen's latest of 13 books is called *Bay Area Wild*.

After photographing for three decades on all seven continents, Yosemite remains as enticing as ever to photograph, and just as unique as when I first saw it as a child. People have told me about a lot of places that are supposed to look like Yosemite, but none have come close. Sure, I've seen higher cliffs, deeper valleys, and countless big waterfalls in the course of my travels, but, like the words of a poem, it's not the individual elements that are poignant, but the way they come together into a meaningful whole.

My mother first arrived in the Valley by open touring car in 1916, during the first year that automobiles were allowed. She fell in love with the park, and in the 1920s performed classical music on summer nights at Camp Curry and the old Glacier Point Hotel. When she introduced me to Yosemite in 1943 at the tender age of three, traffic in the valley wasn't a problem. War time gas rationing was in effect, and no new tires could be purchased. My father saved gas coupons for months, then glued strips of inner tube around his tires to save the treads, taking two full days to make the journey at less than twenty miles per hour.

Regardless of the recent floods of people and water, the essential Yosemite is still 100 percent there for me. I experience it when I'm photographing Half Dome from Ahwahnee Meadow at sunset, when I'm hiking up the Yosemite Falls Trail at dawn, or any time I'm away from the roads in the 96 % of the park that is designated Wilderness.

The rare times that I've been caught in summer traffic jams in the Valley, I've deserved it. I should have planned to have driven there earlier, or to have been out on a remote trail, or to have ridden around the Valley on my bike with my camera pack. There are any number of options to avoid self-imprisonment by seatbelt inside the same mechanized world of vehicles and crowded roads that most visitors seek to leave behind, but never really escape. One survey found average visits to Yosemite lasted two hours with only minutes spent out of a motor vehicle.

Despite the many thousands of photographs I've made in Yosemite over the years, I know I'll never say I've seen it all and put down my camera. I have not *"done"* Yosemite yet, as tourists who collect park stickers are prone to say, because the landscape means more to me than a visual scene to be passively ingested and recorded in snapshots. The Yosemite experience becomes more powerful with each return visit because it is self-renewing, quite unlike the one-time visual exploitation of our senses that happens when we watch an action movie or even a real-life event, such as the Olympic Games, where it's basically all over once the outcome is known. The more you know about the natural world, the more you want to see.

Yosemite has a long history of great interpreters - from John Muir, to Ansel Adams, to the photographers and writers doing the best work today - who have found it necessary to spend long periods of time witnessing the cyclic, but never directly repeated movements of the clouds, the light, the rising mists, and the flowing waters in order to communicate their essential meaning to the public. Thus a guidebook like this should not be shelved after the first flush of familiarity with Yosemite. It needs to be kept handy to savor for new ideas. I'll have my copy of PhotoSecrets beside me on each repeat visit to help me discover ever more moments of serendipity, when the images in my mind and before my eyes can be brought together into inspirational photographs.

Left: *Hiker atop Half Dome, by Galen Rowell.*

PhotoSecrets Yosemite - The Best Sights and How To Photograph Them.
ISBN 978-0-9653087-0-0
First Edition © 1997, reprinted 2002 and 2007.
Author: Andrew Hudson.
Foreword: Galen Rowell.
Designed in the USA; printed in Korea.

PhotoSecrets books are distributed to the trade by National Book Network ☎800-462-6420. For other inquiries contact Photosecrets Publishing ☎800-622-8284.

Publisher's Cataloging in Publication
Hudson, Andrew, 1963-
    PhotoSecrets Yosemite: the best sights and
    how to photograph them / Andrew Hudson.
    p. cm.   Includes index.
    Preassigned LCCN: 97-91459
    ISBN 978-0-9653087-0-0
    1. Yosemite (Calif.)--Guidebooks. 2.
California, Northern--Guidebooks. 3. Travel
photography--Yosemite (Calif.) 4. Travel
photography--California, Northern.   I. Title.
    F867.5.H84 1997   917.94'604'53

Mail: Photo Tour Books, Inc.
        9582 Vista Tercera
        San Diego CA 92129

Visit the web site:
photosecrets.com

Visitors dwarfed by the sheer profile of 'El Cap'.

Photo by Jennie Van Meter

*"Take only photographs,
leave only footprints."*

Thank you for picking up this copy of PhotoSecrets. As a fellow fan of travel and photography, I know this book will help you find the most visually stunning places in Yosemite Valley, and come home with equally stunning photographs.

Ansel Adams created romantic images of Yosemite which will forever influence our view of this unique part of the world. Since *'Monolith'* and *'Clearing Winter Storm'*, The Valley has justly earned the reputation of being a photographer's dreamland. Towering granite cliffs facing the setting sun are laced with a dozen major waterfalls and framed by a luscious landscape. If you enjoy using a camera, you've come to the right place!

PhotoSecrets is designed to quickly show you all the famous 'Ansel Adams' views. As you travel, we'll point out the major landmarks and their history. We'll show you ideas for composition, the best times of day for lighting, and tips for creating your own unique shots. It'll be like travelling with a location scout and a pro-photographer in your pocket.

Now, pack some extra film and follow in the footsteps of Ansel Adams!

Andrew Hudson

CONTENTS

"I *knew* my destiny when I first visited Yosemite."
Ansel Adams, in his autobiography
(available from Little, Brown & Co.)

"Never before had I seen so glorious a landscape."
John Muir

Watching the sunset from Tunnel View.

The Incomparable Valley

Sheer, granite walls, laced with some of the world's tallest waterfalls, tower over verdant fields and the meandering Merced River. The valley is named after it's original indian inhabitants, who white discoverers called the 'Yosemites' after the Miwok name for grizzly bear, 'uzumati'. The indians called the valley 'Ahwahnee' and themselves the 'Ahwahneechees'. Classic 'Ansel Adams' views abound - at every turn there seems something spectacular to photograph. It's an unforgettable sight and justly known as *"The Incomparable Valley"*.

PhotoSecrets Top Ten sights of

Yosemite Valley

Map on following page

Tunnel View
page 14

The most famous 'Ansel Adam's view of Yosemite. From this grand-stand vista you can see El Capitan (left), Half Dome (center), and Bridalveil Falls (right). Great at sunset.

Yosemite Falls
page 18

Over a dozen major waterfalls flow into the valley, but none are taller or more renowned than Yosemite Falls. At 2,425 ft. they are taller than any building. Best viewed in the morning light.

Half Dome
page 22

The highest point in the valley, graceful Half Dome is the symbol of Yosemite. It is best viewed in the early morn-ing and late afternoon.

Bridalveil Fall
page 26

This sheer waterfall changes constantly as it wavers in the wind. Creates wonderful rainbows in the late afternoon.

El Capitan
page 28

Guarding the entrance to the valley, 'El Cap' is the largest known exposed block of granite in the world.

Valley View
page 30

An alternate view to Tunnel View, lesser known but almost as spectacular.

Vernal Fall Trails
page 32

A beautiful hike takes you past Vernal Falls, the popular Mist Trail, Nevada Falls, and, if you're energetic, to the top of Half Dome.

Glacier Point
page 40

A magnificent sky-high view of Half Dome, and the Giant's Staircase of Vernal and Nevada Falls. Only accessible in Summer and Autumn.

Taft Point & Sentinel Dome
page 42

Taft Point is a little-known overlook with stunning views of Half Dome and El Capitan. On the top of Sentinel Dome stands a wind-twisted Jeffrey Pine.

Mirror Lake
page 44

Gradually shrinking Mirror Lake provides calming reflections of Mt. Watkins and Half Dome.

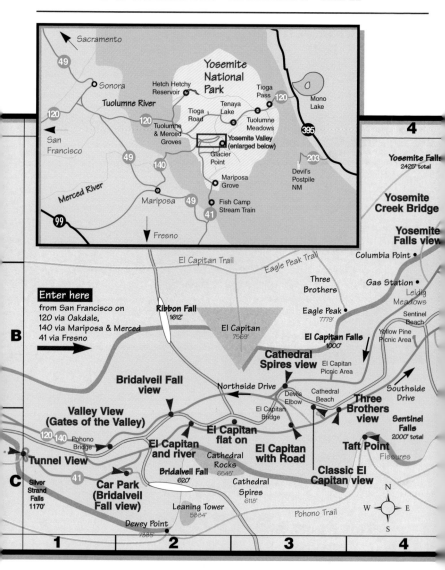

Sacramento

49

Sonora

120

San Francisco

Tuolumne River

Hetch Hetchy Reservoir

120

Tuolumne & Merced Groves

Yosemite National Park

Tioga Road

Tenaya Lake

Tioga Pass

120

Tuolumne Meadows

Mono Lake

395

Yosemite Valley (enlarged below)

Glacier Point

49

140

Merced River

Mariposa

99

49

Mariposa Grove

Fish Camp Stream Train

41

Devil's Postpile NM

203

Fresno

4

Yosemite Falls
2425' total

Yosemite Creek Bridge

Yosemite Falls view

El Capitan Trail

Eagle Peak Trail

Columbia Point •

Enter here
from San Francisco on
120 via Oakdale,
140 via Mariposa & Merced
41 via Fresno

Ribbon Fall
1612'

Three Brothers

Eagle Peak •
7779'

Gas Station •

Leidig Meadows

B

El Capitan
7569'

El Capitan Falls
1000'

Sentinel Beach

Yellow Pine Picnic Area

Cathedral Spires view

El Capitan Picnic Area

Bridalveil Fall view

Northside Drive

Devils Elbow

Cathedral Beach

Southside Drive

Valley View (Gates of the Valley)

El Capitan Bridge

Three Brothers view

Sentinel Falls
2000' total

120 140 Pohono Bridge

El Capitan and river

El Capitan flat on

El Capitan with Road

Taft Point

Fissures

Tunnel View

Cathedral Rocks
6545'

Classic El Capitan view

C

Silver Strand Falls
1170'

41

Car Park (Bridalveil Fall view)

Bridalveil Fall
620'

Cathedral Spires
6118'

Leaning Tower
5884'

Pohono Trail

N
W · E
S

Dewey Point
7385'

1 | **2** | **3** | **4**

Orientation

The only road entrance is from the west. As the trees clear you'll be treated to amazing views of Bridalveil Falls on your right, and Yosemite Falls on your left. Head first to the Visitor Center by turning left at Sentinel Bridge, or go straight on to the day-use parking at Curry Village and use the shuttle bus.

The campgrounds and the most popular trailheads are in the eastern third of the valley. This area is serviced by a free shuttle bus. There is a mostly one-way road system around the valley. You can drive this 14-mile loop, or use the Valley Floor Tram (fee) for a guided tour.

For more information, pick up a copy of the *Yosemite Guide* (free on entry).
Information: ☎209-372-0264.

Legend

Cooks Meadow

Photographic viewpoint.
The circle indicates the location, and the arrow indicates the best viewing direction.

 Major Road

 Minor Road

Pohono Trail Hiking Trail

4 Shuttle Bus Stop

 Rock formation. Number indicates peak elevation above sea level, in feet.

Nevada Fall Waterfall. Number indicates height of the fall, in feet.

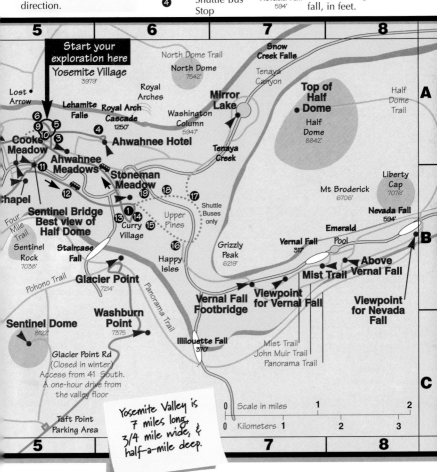

Shuttle Bus Free. Runs every 10 minutes in the Summer daytime.

3 5 6 9 10 Yosemite Village	**8** Yosemite Lodge	**16** Happy Isles
1 14 Curry Village Parking	**11** Sentinel Bridge	**17** Mirror Lake ⎤ No service
2 Upper & Lower River Camps	**12** H'keeping Camp	**18** Stables ⎬ in winter or
4 Ahwahnee Hotel	**15** Upper Pines	**19** Lower Pines ⎦ on summer evenings
7 Yosemite Falls	Campground	Campground

PhotoSecrets Yosemite

Top Ten Sights

Tunnel View is the classic view of Yosemite Valley. From this magnificent vista looking east, up the valley, the main features are spread out in front of you. El Capitan and Bridalveil Falls frame the entrance, with Half Dome standing silently in the distance. It was from near here that in 1944 Ansel Adam's composed his famous photograph, *"Clearing Winter Storm"*. There are many opportunities for you to do the same.

Tunnel view is named after the adjacent Wawona Tunnel (knicknamed the "Whiskey Tunnel" because it is 4/5 of a mile long). The view is also known as **Discovery View** since it greeted the first european visitors, **Best General View**, by 19th century photographers, and **Inspiration Point**, after the nearby peak.

Clearing Winter Storm

I had visualized for many years an image of Yosemite Valley from Inspiration Point and exposed many sheets of film in an effort to achieve that visualization. Finally, in 1944, a sudden heavy rain storm hit, which at midday changed to wet snow.

"I drove to my chosen site and quickly set up my 8x10 camera to capture the marvelous vista spread before me. The clouds were moving rapidly and I waited until the valley was revealed under a mixture of snow and clouds with a silver light, gilding Bridal Veil Fall, realizing the photograph Clearing Winter Storm."

Ansel Adams, in his autobiography.

Where Tunnel View is at the eastern end of the valley, on the road to Fresno and Glacier Point. The Valley Floor Tour bus stops here. If you're driving, take the 'Route 41 Fresno' exit near Bridalveil Falls and drive up the hill. At the entrance to Wawona Tunnel is a large parking area, made of the landfill from the tunnel. You're about 600 feet above the valley floor.

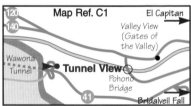

When 🕐 Afternoon is the best time, as the western sun lights the rocks. This is also the best place to watch the sunset.

Watch the rocks change complexion as the sun moves across the sky. At noon, only the southern edge of El Capitan is lit, highlighting it's stark, vertical form. In the late afternoon, with the sun behind you, a rainbow forms at the base of Bridalveil Falls. Around sunset, the golden light graces each feature in turn - El Capitan, then Bridalveil Falls, and finally Half Dome.

The best time of year is Spring and early Summer when cascading Bridalveil Falls is most prominent. In the Winter, the view takes on an otherworldly appearance as clouds hover in the valley.

El Capitan

Clouds Rest   Half Dome

Washington Column   Sentinel Rock (Sentinel Dome is just visible)

Bridalveil Falls Cathedral Rocks

Ansel Adams images from Tunnel View:
- Bridal Veil Fall and Cathedral Rocks, Thunderstorm, c. 1942
- Clearing Winter Storm, 1944
- Yosemite Valley, Moonrise, 1944
- Thunderstorm, Yosemite Valley, 1945

Watching the Sunset

Arrive about two hours before sunset. If you have a tripod, pick a good spot and get set up. At this time, the entire face of El Capitan is nicely lit.

Zoom into El Capitan and capture a nice shot as the sun recedes half way up the face. About 1 hour before sunset, zoom in to Bridalveil Falls, and then to the rocks to your right, as they are warmed by the golden light.

Now zoom in to Half Dome and Cloud's Rest. Just as the sun sets, the sun's final rays create a magical picture (next page). If you're lucky enough to be here a few days before a full moon, just after sunset you could capture the moon rising behind Half Dome.

Above: The unforgettable view from **Tunnel View** ◔ shows most of the main valley features. You can include your companions in the foreground for that *'we are here!'* shot.

Notice how sheer the walls of the valley are. The granite rocks were carved by glaciers - slowly moving rivers of ice - flowing towards this viewpoint.

Far left, below, and following page: Try isolating individual features with a zoom lens. This is a great place to photograph El Capitan (left) and Bridalveil Fall (below).

Cloud's Rest and Half Dome
at sunset from Tunnel View.

"The richest, as well as the most powerful, voice of all the falls in the valley."
John Muir, conservationist.

   Right: *Yosemite Falls plunges almost half a mile from the rim above to meet the flat, verdant valley floor below.*
   Left: *By the Fall season, Yosemite Falls dries to a whispy thread.*

   Ansel Adams images of Yosemite Falls:
   • Lower Yosemite Fall, c. 1946 *(from the Yosemite Creek Bridge viewpoint)*
   • Yosemite Falls and Meadow, 1953 *(from across Cook's Meadow)*

When

The Falls face east so the best time to view them is in the morning. At around 9am the sun lights the plunging water, and is low enough to give relief to the sheer granite walls.

Spring is the best season. Most of the watershed feeding the falls is smooth, bare granite. Unable to store water above, the stream is a torrential storm drain during the snowmelt of April-May, but dries to a whispy thread by August.

In the summer, before 8:30am, hang gliders occasionally glide over from Glacier Point. In the winter, a fascinating cone develops at the base of the Upper, and sometimes Lower, falls as the water freezes on it's descent through the cold air.

In the Spring, white Apple blossoms can provide an interesting foreground during the day, and on a full-moon night, ethereal "moon bows" appear in the lower fall.

   Right: This shot is taken across Cook's Meadow from the **Sentinel Bridge** parking area. Painting and drawing classes come here in the morning, making for an artistic foreground. You can use the reflections in the river as a foreground by standing on the south side of the Merced.

Out of the thirteen waterfalls that feed the valley, none is as awe-inspiring as Yosemite Falls. Plunging a total of 2,425 feet in three sections, Yosemite Falls is taller than any building, and fifteen times the height of Niagara Falls.

Yosemite Falls is composed of three sections, Upper Yosemite Fall (1,430 feet), a middle cascade, and Lower Yosemite Fall. Combined, they form the highest waterfall in North America and the fifth highest in the world.

Yosemite Falls can be seen from many places around the east end of the valley. A good distant view welcomes you from the South Drive as you enter the park.

Where

Yosemite Falls makes a pleasant walk west from the Visitor's Center (see next page). By car, drive west on the Northside Drive towards "Yosemite Exits" to the **parking area** The Shuttle Bus stops here (stop #7), as does the Valley Floor Tour.

From the parking area, a 1/4-mile path leads to the base of the Falls where there is a viewpoint and a **bridge** over Yosemite Creek.

The classic view is taken from the parking area at **Sentinel Bridge** (which also offers a great view of Half Dome). Afterwards follow the **river** west for a great shot over **Cook's Meadow**, then north along Yosemite Creek towards the Falls.

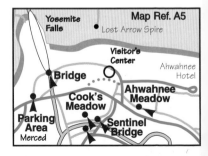

Map Ref. A5

Yosemite Falls • Lost Arrow Spire

Visitor's Center
Ahwahnee Hotel

Bridge

Cook's Meadow

Ahwahnee Meadow

Parking Area
Merced

Sentinel Bridge

*The view from the path on **Ahwahnee Meadows** ☺.*

"The water seems to fall out of the very sky itself." Joseph LeConte, Chief of the US Geological Survey in the west.

Focus On

- Use a slow shutter speed (1/8s) to blur the falling water.

Left: The pathway from the **parking area** leads straight to the falls. It seems designed for your camera. You can create a nicely symmetrical shot, framing the tall, slender falls with the tall, slender trees.

Opposite:
Far Right: Following the path (an easy 10 minute walk) brings you to Yosemite Creek **Bridge**, at the base of the falls. There is a viewpoint here (lower left). The bridge itself makes a delightful foreground, contrasting it's horizontal span with the vertical falls. From the approach side of the bridge, walk gingerly over the rapids to the central section. Be careful of the wet, slippery rocks. It's too rocky for a tripod.

Hiking Up The Falls

Many people's favorite hike takes you up the sheer 2,700 ft. north wall. Start one mile west of the Falls at Sunnyside Campground, behind the gas station near Yosemite Lodge.

One-third of the way up the hike is Columbia Point which has a good view of the top of Lower Yosemite Fall. At the top is a lookout over the entire Yosemite Falls.

Three miles west along the rim is Eagle Point, on top of the Three Brothers rocks. There are spectacular views of the entire Yosemite park, Sierra foothills, and, on a clear day, the Coastal Range far west. If you're camping overnight (permit required) you can hike to the top of El Capitan and return the next day.

3/4 mile east of the falls is Yosemite Point with a view of Lost Arrow Spire, a free-standing shaft of granite.

6-8 hours round trip, very strenuous

Strolling Around The Falls

The best walk in the Valley is around Cook's Meadow to the base of the falls. Start at the Visitor Center and walk south to the river and Sentinel Bridge. Follow the Merced west, then cross the meadow to the base of the falls. Here you can cross the bridge and head back to the Visitor's Center, or return to the parking area and take the Shuttle Bus elsewhere.

1-2 hours roundtrip, easy

alf Dome is the symbol of Yosemite. Standing at the eastern end of the valley, like a father silently guarding his children, Half Dome is the tallest and most recognized rock in Yosemite.

Half Dome is so tall that the glaciers that formed the valley didn't reach the upper 900 feet. Instead, they undermined it's northwest side. Later, when the glacier receded, the rock expanded due to the reduced pressure and then cracked, shearing off the vertically jointed rock layers. This process, called exfoliation, created the Royal Arches and other valley features.

Half Dome is the second sheerest rock wall in the world (the first being in Pakistan). Occasionally climbers can be seen making the five day ascent. A quicker and marginally less strenuous route to the top of Half Dome is a hike up the northeast side, a continuation of the Vernal Fall/ Nevada Fall hike. The 8-mile hike takes 12-14 hours roundtrip and cables allow you to climb the 60° final leg. But the view of the valley floor, 5,000 ft. below, is spectacular.

Where The classic view (right) is taken from **Sentinel Bridge** and is another Ansel Adams classic. The bridge is a 10 minute walk south from Yosemite Village.

When 🕐 Anytime is great. At sunrise and sunset, just the tip of Half Dome is lit in a golden light.

Noon to mid-afternoon is best to capture reflections in the Merced River from Sentinel Bridge. The lowest light on the full scene occurs around 2 hours before sunset.

The river changes with the seasons. In the Spring, it is a fiery torrent. In the Summer, it's host to children and inflatable rafts. In the Autumn and Winter, the calm river offers beautiful reflections.

Ansel Adams images of Half Dome:
- Half Dome, Merced River, Winter, 1938 *(from Sentinel Bridge)*
- Half Dome, Autumn, 1938 *(across Cook's Meadow)*
- Moon and Half Dome, 1960 *(from Stoneman Meadow)*
- Half Dome and Clouds, c. 1968 *(from Glacier Point)*

Left: A popular foreground is the Elm Tree in **Cook's Meadow** ⊕. This is particularly attractive in the winter snow.

Right: The most classic view is from **Sentinel Bridge** ⊕. The pathway provides a great place to set up a tripod and watch the afternoon light affect the view.

Stop here for good photographs

In the Summer you can watch rafters cooling off in the meandering Merced River (next page). In the Fall and Winter, the river becomes placid enough to provide a calming reflection of Half Dome (right).

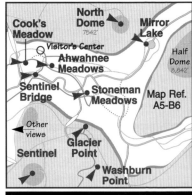

Places to View Half Dome

1	Sentinel Bridge	Classic view
2	Ahwahnee Mdws	Bike path
3	Cook's Meadow	With Elm tree
4	Stoneman Mdws	Natural setting
5	Yosemite Chapel	Good foreground
6	Mirror Lake	Sunrise & sunset
7	Glacier Point	30-mile drive
8	Washburn Point	Profile
9	Tunnel View	With Cloud's Rest
10	Sentinel Dome	Little-known view
11	North Dome	Long hike
12	Highway 120	With El Capitan

The Miwok Indians called Half Dome 'Tis-sa-ock', after a woman whose tear-stained face they saw in the granite.

Above: With Summer rafters, from **Sentinel Bridge** ☺.

Left: Capture the last light of sunset on the sheer face from **Stoneman Meadow** ☺.

Below: The **Chapel** ☺ is a good foreground. This shot is from the center of the meadow, north of Southside Drive.

Above: With El Capitan close to sunset, from a turnout on **Highway 120** ☺ (Big Oak Flat Road).

Below: At **Ahwahnee Meadows** ☺ you can include cyclists in the foreground. Stand on the bike path and wait for people to cycle past. Don't get run over!

*B*ridalveil Fall is considered by many to be the most beautiful of Yosemite's waterfalls. The wind gently sways the whispy waters back and forth as it free-leaps down 620 feet. This motion, called the "Pohono effect", is a delight to watch.

Like Yosemite Falls, Bridalveil is a "hanging valley". It was created when the glaciers widened the main valley, leaving the tributary rivers to flow over a sheer precipice. However, Bridalveil Fall has a larger and more absorbent watershed than Yosemite Falls and remains strong through the Summer.

To the right is Leaning Tower and The Acorn. Behind is Cathedral Rocks.

Ansel Adams images of Bridalveil Fall:
- Bridal Veil Fall, 1927
  (from Tunnel View)
- Bridal Veil Fall and Cathedral Rocks, Thunderstorm, c. 1942
  (from the parking area)

Above: Bridalveil Fall and Leaning Tower from the **Northside Drive Pullout** ⊕
Below: The view from the **parking area** ⊕

Right: A long lens helps you isolate the top of the Fall, with the swirling 'Pohono' effect. Taken from **Northside Drive Pullout**.

Where Bridalveil Falls is at the west end of the valley. The best view is from across the river, at a pullout on the **Northside Drive** ⊕, near Gates of the Valley.

To reach the falls, head for 'Route 41 Fresno'. Just after the turnoff, turn left into the Bridalveil parking area. A 10-minute trail winds up **Bridalveil Creek** . The creek is the best place in the valley to photograph water flowing gently over mossy rocks. Morning sunlight streams through gaps between the maple trees. Set your camera low, near the ferns and logs, and use a long exposure to 'blend' the moving water.

At the top of the trail is a **viewing platform**. The mist is pleasantly cooling in the Summer, but you'll need waterproof clothing in the Spring.

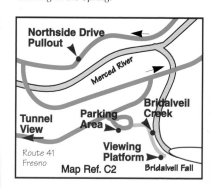

Northside Drive Pullout

Merced River

Tunnel View

Parking Area

Bridalveil Creek

Route 41 Fresno

Viewing Platform ▶

Map Ref. C2   Bridalveil Fall

When 🕐 The real magic of Bridalveil is watching how the changing light affects the Fall's appearance. In the mid-morning, when sunlight first strikes the Fall, it highlights just the water cresting the rim. Get set up beforehand, zoom-in (200mm with tripod), and wait for the right moment to capture the golden sliver of spray. In the late-afternoon, the swirling mist and the light from the low sun create thick, dramatic rainbows at the base. Both shots are best taken from the west end of the **parking area** ⊕. Shortly before sunset, the granite rock face turns golden with the light of the setting sun.

In Spring, the heavy mist makes it almost impossible to photograph from the base. In Winter, various cones and shapes are formed by the frozen water.

E**l Capitan,** spanish for "the chief", guards the entrance to Yosemite Valley. This giant monolith, rising 3,593 ft. above the meandering Merced River, is thought to be the largest single block of exposed granite in the world.

On the west side is **Ribbon Fall**, the highest single waterfall in Yosemite National Park. With a descent of 1,612 ft. it is also one of the highest in the world. On the east side, during late winter and early spring, is **Horsetail Fall**. This photographs well in the late-afternoon as the sun shines through the whispy spray.

When ⏰ Anytime is fine although the late afternoon turns the granite face a burning orange color. A good shot from **Valley View** ⏰ (*Gates of the Valley*) occurs 1-2 hours before sunset when the sun lights just the top half of the rock face.

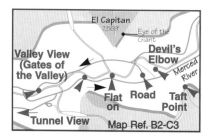

"The great rocks of Yosemite, expressing qualities of timeless, yet intimate grandeur... are the very heart of the earth speaking to us." Ansel Adams

Ansel Adams images of El Capitan:
- El Capitan from Taft Point, c. 1936 (*from Taft Point*)
- El Capitan, 1952 (*from Devil's Elbow*)
- El Capitan, Winter, Sunrise, 1968 (*from Devil's Elbow*)

Left: Ansel Adams' favorite view of El Capitan was from **Devil's Elbow** ⏰, near Cathedral Beach. The east face is fully lit by the morning sun, but by late afternoon the distinctive profile is highlighted and more prominent. Winter is particularly attractive as clouds drift across the 3,245 ft. monolith.

There is a small turnout on the Southside Drive with a sign describing the seven different types of granite prevalent in the valley. Walk down to the banks of the Merced and follow the river east for about 50 yards so that the river completely fills the bottom of the frame.

In the Summer canoeists occasionally paddle by, adding human interest and an important sense of scale.

Below: Sunset on El Capitan. This classic shot is taken from **Tunnel View** ⏰.

Above: The leading lines of the **road** draw your eye into the deep, immense background. *Below:* Facing El Capitan **flat on** ☉, from south of the river, shows you how incredibly sheer and perpendicular it's walls are. From a tiny pullout on Southside Drive, walk north to the river's edge.

Above: The most popular view of El Capitan is from **Valley View** ☉ (also called *Gates of the Valley*). You can use reflections in the river (placid in Fall and Winter) for a foreground. This is a popular view in the winter as snow clumps on the river's rocks, and access is easy.

There's a great temptation to use a wide-angle lens and include Bridalveil Fall, but fight it and isolate El Capitan. Crouch down low at the edge of the water to bring the river through the bottom of the frame.

Below: El Capitan is a haven for climbers. Bring a pair of binoculars to go climber-spotting. Popular routes are the *North American Wall* and the *Wall of the Early Morning Light* which can be best seen at *Eye of the Giant*. You can watch from the base although a more scenic viewpoint is from Taft Point.

The view from Valley View (also known as **Gates of the Valley**) rivals the power of that from Tunnel View, but is far less photographed. It's also a more tranquil spot to watch the last rays of the setting sun move from left to right, as if being covered by a slowly drawn curtain. You can clearly see El Capitan (left), Cathedral Rocks and Bridalveil Fall (to the right).

The river here flows across the shot, forming a unifying foreground. Crouch low to bring the water almost to eye level.

Ansel Adams images from Valley View:
• Gates of the Valley, Winter, c. 1938

Tip This view makes an excellent panoramic shot. If you don't have a panoramic camera, don't worry. Take a normal shot then, when you get the photographs developed, ask for a 8"x10" enlargement. Crop off the top and bottom 2.5 inches, and you'll be left with a 10" x 3" panorama.

When 🕐 The west facing rocks look best in the afternoon light. Bridalveil Fall is most prominent in the Spring. In the Winter, clumps of snow form on the boulders in the river making this one of the best views in the Valley.

"We finally emerged at Valley View - the splendor of Yosemite burst upon us and it was glorious."
Ansel Adams

Where Valley View is a turnout from the north exit road at the end of the valley. The Valley Floor Tram stops here but if you're driving you'll need a quick eye as the turnout is almost hidden by a bend in the road. Take the Northside Drive. 4.2 miles from the gas station. Just after you see the sign for 41 Wawona/Fresno, by Marker V-11, the pullout is on your left.

"As I looked, a peculiar exalted sensation seemed to fill my whole being, and I found my eyes in tears with emotion."
Lafayette Bunnell, on first 'discovering' Yosemite.

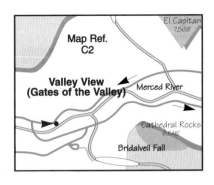

The Merced River was named in 1806 by Sergeant Gabriel Moraga, a Spanish explorer. His party had traveled over forty miles with no water and were overjoyed to find the river. They called it "The River of Our Lady of Mercy" - *"El Rio de Nuestra Senora de la Merced"*.

"The Vernal Fall I so named because of the cool, vernal spray in contrast at midday with summer heat, reminding me of an April shower, and because of the blue grass curiously growing among dark rocks and gay, dripping flowers, making it an eternal April to the ground."
Lafayette Bunnell, 1851.

Ansel Adams images along the Vernal Fall trails.
• Nevada Fall, Rainbow, 1946 *(from north trail)*
• Nevada Fall, Profile, c. 1946 *(from north trail)*
• Vernal Fall, c. 1948 *(from viewpoint)*

Left: Vernal Fall is 317 ft. high and 80-100 ft. wide at it's Spring peak. The classic view is from a signposted area, the **Vernal Fall viewpoint** ☉, along the Mist trail. A granite outcrop provides a stable platform.

Right: The most impressive view of Vernal Fall is from the **trail cutoff** ☉ above Emerald Pool. This short trail connects the Mist Trail to the John Muir Trail. Here the full power of the cascading Merced river is apparent.

Of the 840 miles of hiking paths in Yosemite National Park, the most scenic are those up Little Yosemite Valley to Vernal Fall and Nevada Fall. You can make a short hike to the base of Vernal Fall (which offers the most photo opportunities), spend an afternoon continuing on to Nevada Fall, or spend a 1-2 day trip hiking to the top of Half Dome.

When ⏱ Afternoon is the best time for light as both Falls face west. Because the Merced River drains the large absorbent Tuolumne Meadows above, the Falls remain active throughout the dry summer months. In the Spring, parts of the trail are wet, and in Winter watch for slippery ice.

Where The trails start at Shuttle Stop 16. This area is called Happy Isles for the two small islands in the Merced River where it enters Yosemite Valley. Note that the bus doesn't run during the winter, or in the summer evenings - you'll need to walk to/from Curry Village.

The path starts on the east bank of the river and is signposted to Vernal Falls and the John Muir Trail'. From Nov-May, the higher elevations may be impassable due to snow.

Put your camera in a plastic, zip-lock bag to protect it from the spray.

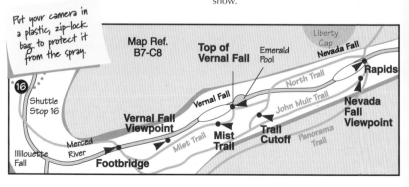

Above: The view from the **footbridge** 🕐 below Vernal Fall. The fresh spring foliage of white alder, black cottonwood, bigleaf maple, and western azalea, decorate the banks of the Merced River. Overcast, cloudy weather will reduce the contrast of the scene and bring out the verdant greens.

Preparation

In Spring and early Summer it's steep and wet up there. Bring a rainproof jacket and wrap your camera, batteries, and film in a plastic bag. Bring a small towel and cloths to wipe spray from the lens. A backpack is better than a shoulder bag as it balances your upper body and keeps your hands free for walking.

Left: A hundred yards from the bridge is the **Vernal Fall viewpoint** 🕐 (signposted) A large granite boulder provides a sturdy support for your tripod. Bring a lens-cleaning tissue or cloth to keep the lens free of water droplets.

Tip The glorious rapids which pass by will tempt you to use a wide-angle lens to include everything. But this will detract from your main subject. Instead, try a 70mm lens and emphasize the Fall.

Focus On

* Watch for rainbows in the afternoon
* Include hikers for a sense of scale

"Nature's peace will flow into you as sunshine flows into trees." John Muir

Hiking

Base of Vernal Fall. *Roundtrip: 1-2 hours*
A reasonably strenuous 30 minute hike takes you past Illilouette Fall to Vernal Fall. A bridge over the river makes a good viewpoint, but the classic view is 100 yards further on (go left at the trail junction to the signposted "View"). This exposed rock makes a good platform for tripods.

Top of Vernal Fall. *Roundtrip: 2-4 hours*
Continue on the aptly named 'Mist Trail'. Hiker's in the Spring get soaked as they walk past the base of the Fall but it's fun, and the lush vegetation and outstanding view from the top are worth it. The alternative 'John Muir Trail' is a dryer but longer route.

Nevada Fall. *Roundtrip: 4-6 hours*
Follow the river uphill. Just before the bridge the path splits. The path crossing the bridge is shorter and steeper but not as scenic. Instead go right, uphill, and rejoin the John Muir Trail. There are several views of Nevada Fall but the best is where the path straightens out along an overhang. There's a small wall here.

Half Dome. *Roundtrip 10-12 hours*
Continue along the river around to the east side of Half Dome. The last 200 yards are so steep that a steel cable handrails are provided for assistance. You'll need gloves and good shoes on this section. In the Summer, about 600 people a day make the ascent. A one day trip provides little time to enjoy the view, if you can, stay overnight by camping about a mile above Nevada Fall. A permit and bear-proof food storage is required.

The popular **Mist Trail** is a 1-mile long slippery route through the spray of Vernal Fall. In the Spring, intrepid (or foolhardy) hikers are drenched as they race through the luxuriant vegetation and descending spray.

Above: It's a brave person who snaps this shot as the spray can ruin a camera (*mine stopped afterward and I had to return back to get a replacement!*). Use a waterproof camera, or a clear plastic bag stretched over, or cut around, the lens.

Next page: The Miwoks called Vernal Fall 'Yan-o-pah', meaning *'little cloud'*, after the enormous spray it generated. In 1897, a 300-foot granite staircase, called the Mist Trail, was carved into the rock, winding it's way through the *little cloud.*

A quote by the Vernal Fall Viewpoint.

"...rocky strength and permanence combined with beauty of plants frail and fine... water descending in thunder, and the same water gliding through meadows and groves in gentlest beauty."

John Muir

The luscious **Mist Trail** glows like an exotic land in the Spring. This shot is best in the late afternoon, facing west into the setting sun.

Twelve Highest Waterfalls

		Height in feet
1	Yosemite Falls	2,425
2	Sentinel Falls	2,000
3	Ribbon Fall	1,612
4	Staircase Falls	1,300
5	Royal Arch Cascade	1,250
6	Silver Strand Falls	1,170
7	El Capitan Falls	1,000
8	Lehamite Falls	800
9	Bridalveil Fall	620
10	Nevada Fall	594
11	Illilouette Fall	370
12	Vernal Fall	317

Left: At the **top of Vernal Fall** is a viewpoint only inches from the edge. Use a wide-angle lens (24mm) to include a peron in the foreground to complement the far background.

Lower Left: From the **Mist Trail** ⌚ you can catch rainbows at the base of the fall. Rainbows occur when the sun is directly behind you.

Right: Where the famous John Muir Trail runs under an overhanging rock, a small safety wall provides a good **Nevada Fall viewpoint** ⌚. Here you can see the 594 ft. Nevada Fall with the 7,076 ft. Liberty Cap behind.

Below: At the brink of the fall, you can see the raw, tempestuous power of the Merced River as is is forced through a narrow chute. A small bridge has good views of the **rapids** ⌚ before the chute.

The Giant's Staircase

As opposed to the "hanging valleys" of Yosemite and Bridalveil Falls where the glaciers sliced across the river, Vernal and Nevada Falls were formed when glaciers moved down the river. The huge pressures cracked the rock along natural fault lines, dislodging large blocks of granite, and creating two major steps. This effect earns Little Yosemite Valley the nickname of "The Giants' Staircase". It is most apparent from Glacier Point.

"With Yosemite, we have one of the most extraordinary places on earth, but Yosemite possesses a "Fatal beauty" which invites self-destruction unless we make a strenuous effort to control visitation and use."

Ansel Adams in a radio address, 1968.

"I long for the high places - they are so clean and pure and untouched."
Ansel Adams in a letter to Virginia Best, March 30, 1923.

Ansel Adams images from Glacier Point.
• Half Dome and Clouds, c. 1968

Left: From **Glacier Point** ☻ you have a great view of Half Dome. In 1973, the entertainment company MCA planned to put a gondola from the valley floor up to Glacier Point.

When ⏱ The afternoon offers the best light, but be sure to come here at sunset for the last light on Half Dome.

Winter Only: Snow closes the road between November and May, when it becomes a popular destination for cross-country skiers.

Summer Only: On weekend mornings (before 8am), hang gliders occasionally leap from Glacier Point and swoop to the valley below. There is a large telescope on Glacier Point and rangers provide evening astronomy programs.

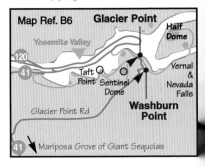

Glacier Point offers the most dramatic overlook in the Sierra Nevada. From here you have a commanding view of Yosemite Valley, Half Dome, and the High Sierra with its rugged ridges, glaciated canyons and serrated summits. Mt. Lyell, the highest point in the park, is behind Nevada Fall. On the valley floor, 3,214 ft.below, cars look like toys and people look like ants.

Afterwards, head to Sentinel Dome and Taft Point, Mariposa Grove, or hike along the rim.

Where Glacier Point is a 32-mile, 1-hour drive from the Valley floor. Take the 'Route 41 Fresno' exit through Wawona Tunnel, then left on Glacier Point Road. The Valley Floor Tour does not go here but the Glacier Point Tour does. In the Summer there is an evening Kodak Photo Tour.

The adventurous can take a 3-4 hour hike from the valley floor up Four Mile Trail (actually 4.8 miles). The trail starts on Southside Drive, one mile west of Yosemite Village by Sentinel Rock. An alternate route is the Panorama Cliffs Trail (6-8 hours, 8.5 miles), past Vernal and Nevada Falls.

The adventurous-but-wise can take the Hiker's Bus to Glacier Point and hike down instead of up the trails.

"If you were to give me the pleasure of showing you Yosemite Valley for the first time, I know just how I would want to do it. I would take you by night from the San Joaquin Valley up through the forested mountains and out to the Valley's rim, so that when sunrise came you would be standing on Glacier Point. Up before dawn, you would lean against the railing, trying to see down into the shadows for the first sight of something whose descriptions you never quite believed."
Ansel Adams, in 'Travel and Camera', October, 1946.

Above: Glacier Point offers aerial views of most of the valley features. You can see Mount Lyell, the tallest peak in the park, at 13,114'. Mt. Lyell is home to one of the two glaciers which still remains in the park.

Below left: Use a telephoto lens to isolate the 'Giants Staircase' of Nevada Falls (top) and Vernal Falls (below).

Below right: This is an excellent place to watch the sunset. In the fleeting last minutes of sun, the granite glows a golden brown. You'll need 210mm lens and a tripod to get a sharp photograph. This shot was taken from nearby **Washburn Point** ⓒ.

H alf way along **Glacier Point Road** are two notable hikes that share the same trailhead. One mile east brings you to the summit of Sentinel Dome with it's famous Jeffrey Pine, and a similar distance west takes you to the overhanging viewpoint of Taft Point.

Where Start at the parking area on Glacier Point Road, marked by a sign and some bathrooms.

When 🕐 Anytime is fine. A low light is preferred to bring out the depth of the valley (at midday the scene looks flat).

Glacier Point Road is closed in the Winter (Nov-Mar).

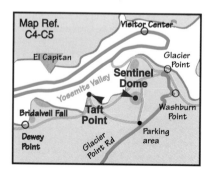

Map Ref.
C4-C5

Ansel Adams images from Taft Point:
• El Capitan from Taft Point, c. 1936

from Sentinel Dome:
• Jeffrey Pine, Sentinel Dome, 1940

Taft Point Map Ref. C4
1-2 hours

This little-visited area is one of the 'Secrets' of Yosemite. A mostly flat 1.1 mile trail leads through delightful woods. In the Spring, a carpet of colorful wild flowers surrounds you. Near Taft Point are huge fissures - gaps in the rock which are a few feet wide and hundreds of feet deep. But this is just a teaser for the main event. At Taft Point, the granite abruptly stops in an almost sheer vertical drop. Standing on the overhang, there's nothing between you and the valley floor, over 3,000 ft. below.

Bring a pair of binoculars. Across the valley is El Capitan and this is a great place to have lunch and spot the miniscule climbers creeping up it's face.

Tip Fortunately there are actually two overlooks at Taft Point. Stand at the railings and look west (left) to the second overlook. Include your companions standing on the edge - if they're brave enough!

Below: For a sense of scale, that's me in orange on the overhang!

"A sturdy storm-enduring mountaineer of a tree, living on sunshine and snow, maintain tough health on this diet for perhaps more than a thousand years."
John Muir

Sentinel Dome   Map Ref. C5
1-2 hours

After Half Dome, Sentinel Dome is the highest point in Yosemite Valley. From the 8,122 ft. high peak you have a glorious 360-degree view across the park. This is a great panorama at any time, but sunrise, sunset, and full moon nights offer artistic opportunities.

Most of the elevation is covered by car leaving only a 30 minute moderate walk from the parking area to the peak. This is a relief for anyone with a heavy tripod or large-format camera.

The most fascinating feature of Sentinel Dome is a lone **Jeffrey Pine**, poised on the summit. For several hundred years this tree grew from the cracks of seemingly barren rock, but it died in the drought of 1979. Now a stark, eerie form, it provides a unique subject.

Sentinel Dome is almost 1,000 feet higher than Glacier Point but unfortunately doesn't offer a view of Yosemite Valley.

Above: The wind-twisted Jeffrey Pine on Sentinel Dome is considered one of the most photographed trees in the world.

Top Ten Highest Peaks

		Height in feet
1	Mt Lyell	13,114
2	Mt Dana	13,053
3	Rodgers Peak	12,978
4	Mt Maclure	12,764
5	Mt Gibbs	12,764
6	Mt Conness	12,590
7	Mt Florence	12,561
8	Simmons Peak	12,503
9	Excelsior Mountain	12,446
10	Electra Peak	12,442

"The entire Yosemite Valley is the supreme concentration of grandeur and beauty."
Ansel Adams, Architectural Record, February, 1957.

Nearby
Dewey Point

Dewey Point (7,385 ft.) offers interesting views of El Capitan and Bridalveil Fall. The trail head is also on Glacier Point Road, just west of the Bridalveil Campground. This is an easy hike with little elevation change but a roundtrip distance of 7 miles make it a 4-6 hour hike.

Mirror Lake was once a large body of water with a mirror-like surface. Some terrific photographs were taken here, particularly in Winter, with reflections of Half Dome. However, the lake is naturally filling with silt and has all but disappeared. Many a hiker asks *'Is this it?'* and leaves disillusioned. So catch it while you can!

From this soon-to-be meadow there are good views of Half Dome, Mount Watkins and Basket Dome. It's a pleasant hike up Tenaya Creek.

Where

Start at Shuttle Bus stop #17. In winter this stop is not accessible so you have to walk from the Pines Campground, stop #19. The lake is a pleasant easy half-mile walk up Tenaya Creek. This is a popular destination by bike.

When 🕐

Early morning or sunset is the best time.

Winter and Spring are the best seasons as the lake can dry up by Summer. The most romantic view is probably sunset in Winter.

In the Spring, Tenaya Creek is lined with dogwood, making for beautiful nature photographs.

"Yosemite is one of the great gestures of the earth. It isn't that it is merely big - it is also beautiful, with a beauty that is as solid and apparent as the granite rock in which it is carved."

Ansel Adams in a letter to Alfred Stieglitz, November, 1937.

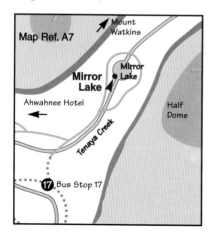

"Yosemite Valley, to me, is always a sunrise, a glitter of green and golden wonder in a vast edifice of stone and space."
Ansel Adams

Right: Idyllic Mirror Lake reflects the distant Mount Watkins.

Ansel Adams images of Mirror Lake:
• Mirror Lake, Mount Watkins, Spring, 1935
(from the west bank of the lake, facing Mount Watkins)

Making the Valley

Mirror Lake is a living example of how the flat Yosemite Valley floor was formed.

Millions of years ago, the Tenaya Creek and Merced River carved a deep 'V'-shaped valley. Later, one-and-a-half million years ago, the rivers turned to ice, forming glaciers (slowly moving rivers of ice) and gouged the lower levels of the valley into a distinctive 'U' shape. (Two glaciers still exist in the park). Waterfalls were created as the widening valley became lower than the tributary rivers, leaving "Hanging Valleys".

Near El Capitan, large rocks formed a dam and turned the valley into a lake. Gradually silt accumulated, filling up the lake, just as Mirror Lake is now. Sediment collected to a depth of 2,000 feet in 6,000 years. Eventually the lake disappeared altogether, replaced with a flat, fertile valley floor.

Mirror Lake is following the same process. Soon, the lake will disappear altogether and the area will become a meadow.

"The silver light turned every blade of grass and every particle of sand into a luminous metallic splendor; there was nothing, however small, that did not clash in the bright wind, that did not send arrows of light through the glassy air. I was suddenly arrested in the long crunching path up the ridge by an exceedingly pointed awareness of the light... I saw more clearly than I have ever seen before or since."
Ansel Adams in Yosemite and the High Sierra.

PhotoSecrets Yosemite

Other Sights

Ahwahnee Hotel   Map Ref.A6

Left: Opened in 1927, The Ahwahnee is one of the most beautiful hotels in America. Built from native stone and wood, it blends with the sheer granite rocks behind. Even the concrete beams are stained to look like redwood. The Ahwahnee has housed Presidents, royalty and celebrities, and has been designated a National Historic Landmark.

The elegant dining room is flooded with sunlight through the massive 34-foot high floor-to-ceiling windows. Some have called it the most beautiful restaurant in America. To eat dinner here, jackets are required, as are reservations (☎209-372-1489 or, from your room, ext. 1304).

Ahwahnee is the Miwok name for the Yosemite Valley. It means "place of the gaping mouth". This shot is taken from the gardens behind the hotel.

Ansel Adams images:
- Sentinel Rock and Clouds, Winter, c. 1937
- North Dome, Royal Arches, Washington Column, Winter, c. 1940
- Cathedral Rocks, c. 1949
- Eagle Peak and Middle Brother, Winter, c. 1960
- Fern Spring, Dusk, c. 1960

Sentinel Rock   Map Ref.B5

Far left: Jagged Sentinel ("guarding soldier") Rock is 7,038 feet high and anchors the south side of the valley. This shot is taken from a meadow near Northside Drive.

Chapel   Map Ref.B5

Near left: Built in 1879, this Chapel was originally part of a small town built on the valley floor. The other structures have since been demolished and the area restored, but the Chapel was relocated in 1901 and still hosts worship services and weddings. It is a short walk from Sentinel Bridge on the south road.

The Chapel makes a good foreground to Half Dome, but it's a challenge to fit the two together. This shot is taken from center of the meadow, north of Southside Drive.

Royal Arches   Map Ref.A6

Above: Behind and to the east of the Ahwahnee Hotel is this unusual rock pattern. Leaves of rock fell away (a process called 'exfoliation') leaving these Royal Arches. To the right stands Washington Column and behind is North Dome.

This shot is taken from Stoneman Meadow and benefits from the late afternoon sun.

Three Brothers   Map Ref.B3

Right: Just east of El Capitan are the distinctive slopes of Three Brothers. The apex,

Eagle Peak, can be reached from the top of the Yosemite Falls trail. The three peaks are named after the three sons of Tenaya, the last chief of the Ahwahneechee.

This shot is from Cathedral Beach, near Devil's Elbow. There is a small parking area on Southside Drive (with an information board about granite in the valley), just after the cutoff to El Capitan. Walking west allows you to include the reflecting Merced River in the foreground. A little further west is the classic view of El Capitan.

Sequoias and Redwoods

The Coast Redwood and the Giant Sequoia (Sierra Redwood) are relatives with slight differences. The Sequoia has a spongier, cinnamon-colored bark while the Redwood has a thinner, orange/gray bark. The Redwood is thinner and taller since, once a Sequoia has reached a certain height, its growth is *outward*. Both trees were once widespread throughout the world but, for some reason, have retreated to grow only on opposite sides of California's Great Valley, one tree as the largest living thing and the other as the tallest.

Where   **Mariposa Grove** is 36 miles (1 hr 15) south of Yosemite Valley via Rt. 41. It is popular in the Summer so visit before 10am or after 3pm. Overflow parking is located in Wawona with a free shuttle service. The grove can be closed in Winter.

There are two other groves in the park (both near Crane Flat) but they are not as large and accessible. **Tuolumne Grove** has more trees including the **Dead Giant**, a 40' stump with an automobile tunnel (but cars are no longer allowed through it) and the **Siamese Twins** (two trees which grew close together and unite to be 114' in circumference). **Merced Grove** has 20 trees and requires a two-mile strenuous hike. There are only 75 Sequoia groves in California.

Mariposa Grove of Giant Sequoias is the finest strand of giant sequoias outside of Sequoia National Park (5 hours south). Giant Sequoias are the world's largest trees, in fact the world's largest lifeform, and are only found in a small belt of the Sierra Nevada.

Inside the park there are several interesting specimens. Grizzly Giant is thought to be the oldest living sequoia at 2,700 years. The 232' California Tree has a pedestrian tunnel through it's trunk, cut in the 1800's. You can stand inside Telescope Tree and see the sky through the top. There was a tree that you could drive a car through, the Wawona Tree, but this collapsed from a weakened base.

Clothespin Tree has an open trunk, caused by fire.

Wawona Point (view) 6,810 ft

Galen Clark Tree

Mariposa Tree

Columbia Tree   Museum

Wawona Tunnel Tree (fallen)

Clothespin Tree

Faithful Couple

Telescope Tree

Hiking path

California Tunnel Tree

From Yosemite Valley and Wawona

Bachelor and Three Graces

Grizzly Giant

From the Parking Area to the Museum is 2.1 miles and 800' elevation gain.

Parking Area

Fallen Monarch

Tram starts here

Tram stop

Tram route

OUTSIDE THE VALLEY

Yosemite Valley occupies only 5% of Yosemite National Park. Most of the remainder is reached by Tioga Road.

Originally built in 1883 as a wagon road for a silver mining company, Tioga Road (Highway 120) passes forests, wide open meadows and sparkling blue lakes. There are frequent turnouts offering broad, beautiful panoramas. In the summer the wildflowers bloom and the resident climbers relocate here from Yosemite Valley.

At 9,945 feet, Tioga (pronounced 'Tie-o-ga') Pass is the highest automobile pass in California and the drive up, carved out of a nearly vertical cliff, can be demanding.

Because of the elevation, the road closes with the first major snowstorm, and doesn't open again until most of the snow has thawed. The road is usually open from June to October although chains may be required in June, September and October. A hiker's bus operates from July 1 to Labor Day (☎209-372-1240).

Wawona

The Pioneer History Center transports you back to the late 1800's. There is a New England-style covered bridge and a collection of stage coaches and in the Summer, the staff wear Victorian costumes.

The elegant Wawona Hotel, built in 1875, is a magnificent white building with neatly mown grass, deck chairs and a golf course. A fountain in front provides a good foreground.

Hetch Hetchy Reservoir

Once-upon-a-time this was a beautiful waterfall-graced valley similar to Yosemite Valley. From 1919 to 1923 a large concrete dam was built, turning the area into a large reservoir. Hetch Hetchy now provides most of the water and power for San Francisco. The water flows 200 miles from here to the city purely by gravity.

You can photograph O'Shaughnessy Dam with Tueeulala and Wapama waterfalls in the distance. Hetch Hetchy is fed by the Tuolumne River, from Tuolumne Meadows, and is named after the Miwok word for an edible grass.

Olmstead Point

Olmstead Point has a great, although distant, view of Half Dome. Several round boulders provide a popular foreground. They were deposited here by the glaciers and are called "Glacial Erratics".

The point was named after Frederick Law Olmstead who designed New York's Central Park and was appointed Chairman of the Yosemite Valley Commissioners.

Tenaya Lake

Tenaya (pronounced 'ten-eye-a') Lake is a beautiful and large alpine lake. It was named in 1851 by the Mariposa Battalion to honor the Chief of the Yosemite Miwoks, Tenaya. The Miwoks called the lake "Py-wi-ock" or "Lake of the Glistening Rocks".

Tuolumne Meadows

"The Tuolumne Meadow is a beautiful grassy plain of great extent, thickly enameled with flowers, and surrounded with the most magnificent scenery."
Joseph LeConte.

Tuolumne (pronounced 't-wolo-me') Meadow is the largest sub-alpine meadow in the Sierra Nevada. Wide, verdant meadows are laced with mountain springs and surrounded by stark, snow-topped peaks. At an elevation of 8,575' above sea level, it can be buried in 20' drifts of snow in the winter but, in the summer, it is a peaceful haven from the busy valley. The mountain air is fresh and wildflowers abound. Fed by the winding Tuolumne River, this is a beautiful area for hiking and photography.

Tuolumne Meadows is 55 miles from Yosemite Valley. From the Visitor Center, trailheads lead to the major sights.

Lakes and Peaks

From behind Tuolumne Meadows Campground, a 2.3 mile trail takes you to Unicorn Peak and Elizabeth Lake. With elegant Unicorn Peak in the background, the lake makes one of the most attractive photos in the area. Another popular hike is 3.5 miles to Cathedral Lake. The trail starts from the parking area west of the Visitor Center.

Waterwheel Falls

A long hike (8-10 hours roundtrip) is rewarded by Waterwheel Falls, one of a series of cascades. The river smashes into granite shelves, sending enormous arcs of water skyward, and down the 5,000 foot-deep chasm.

The best time for viewing is mid-June through mid-July. Waterwheel Falls is 6 miles NW of the Tuolumne Meadows Ranger Station along the Pacific Coast Trail.

OUTSIDE THE PARK

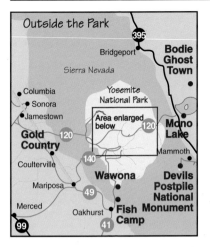

Outside the Park

South Tufa Reserve is the best place for photography, particularly at dawn. There are volcanic craters nearby. ☎619-647-3044.

Devils Postpile

Hot lava has cracked into 60' tall geometric towers in this ancient valley. Nearby are several waterfalls. Access is via Mammoth Lakes. Closed in winter.

Bodie Ghost Town

This is the most photogenic ghost town in California. In a remote location stand 80 buildings, several with their original contents still visible through the windows, all preserved in a state of 'arrested decay'. The stark landscape and weathered textures are a playground for black and white photographers. At 8,000' elevation, Bodie can become inaccessible in the Winter. ☎619-647-6445.

Fish Camp

A preserved logging steam train takes visitors through the woods. Closed in winter.

The Gold Country

Over 200 Victorian gold mining towns are strung along historic Route 49. Coulterville, Jamestown and Columbia State Historic Park are good stops.

Surrounding Yosemite Valley is an area of natural wonders and photogenic gold-mining towns.

Mono Lake

In 1941 the City of Los Angeles started draining this ancient lake to supply water to the city. As the water level dropped, strange 'Tufa' (pronounced 'two-fah') formations were revealed. These knobbly towers had been formed as mineral-rich springs bubbled through the alkaline water. The

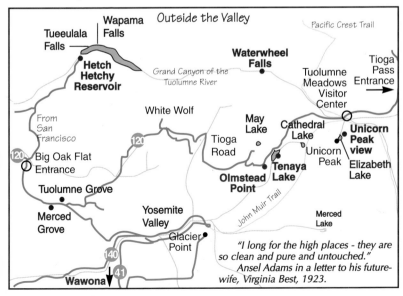

"I long for the high places - they are so clean and pure and untouched."
Ansel Adams in a letter to his future-wife, Virginia Best, 1923.

The Whistlestop Tour

Yosemite Valley requires at least three days but if one is all you have, here's a suggested itinerary.

When you first arrive, head for **Yosemite Village** which has information, restaurants, and reservations. Find the **Visitor's Center** (open 9-5pm/8-6pm, Shuttle Stops 6 & 9) for a good orientation. There are displays showing the formation of the valley, lots of guide books, and enthusiastic rangers to offer advice.

The best overview is on the **Valley Floor Tour** ($14, from Yosemite Village), a guided, two-hour trip to the main sights on an open-air tram. It stops at most of the main sights including **Yosemite Falls**, **El Capitan**, Sentinel Bridge (for a view of **Half Dome**), **Gates of the Valley**, and **Tunnel View**. Alternatively you can drive this 8.5 mile loop. There probably won't be time but Glacier Point (1-2 hours) has spectacular aerial views of almost the entire valley.

In the afternoon hike to either Yosemite Fall (1-2 hrs) or Vernal Fall (2-4 hrs).

Yosemite Fall makes for a very relaxing walk. Start at the Visitor Center and head south to Sentinel Bridge. Follow the river east, then head north to the Fall. From the base of the Fall, a path leads back to the Visitor Center.

A more strenuous but equally spectacular hike is to **Vernal Fall**. Take the Shuttle to Happy Isles at stop 16. Budget 3 hours total for a moderate hike to the base of the falls. If you enjoy getting wet, hike to the top of the falls on the popular **Mist Trail** (4 hours total). Extending on to **Nevada Fall** (go up the southern John Muir Trail and return down the north trail) adds two more hours which is just possible for the quick of feet in the long days of Summer.

The best place to watch the sunset is **Tunnel View**. Also try **Glacier Point**, **Stoneman Meadow** and **Gates of the Valley**.

Getting There

By Car: The quickest route from San Francisco (4-5hrs, 195 miles) is on Route 120 via I-580 and Oakdale. Route 140 via Mariposa follows the Merced River and is a more scenic and gentler climb (may be closed due to Jan '97 floods). Southerners can take Route 41 via Fresno and Oakhurst.

By Bus or Train: Get to Merced or Fresno and take the Yosemite Gray Line bus (800-345-4950 in CA, or 209-383-1563) or a private tour bus (☎209-384-2576, 209-443-5240, or 209-372-1240).

Getting Around

As you enter the park, pick up the free *Yosemite Guide* for information on tours, photography walks and other activities. A free shuttle bus operates all year around the Valley floor, and from Wawona to Mariposa Grove (Spring to Fall). Hiker's buses go to Glacier Point (late spring through fall) and Tuolumne Meadows (late June through Labor Day). Call 209-372-1240, or a hotel tour desk. A wide range of sightseeing tours, with informed guides, are available ($14 - $38.50, ☎209-372-1240).

Staying There

Accommodation in the valley is limited. There are four camp grounds ($3-$14) but reservations are often necessary (☎800-436-7275 or 619-452-8787). The only walk-in camp ground is Sunnyside. The nights get cool in the summer, and downright freezing in winter. For the tentless, there are four lodges (☎209-252-4848) and, if it's someone else's credit card, the $215 a night Ahwahnee Hotel. Additional camp sites are by the south entrance, near Wawona and at the western entrance in Hodgdon Meadow. There are B&B's 30 minutes away at Yosemite West and motels about an hour away in Oakhurst (South), El Portal, Mariposa, Sonora and Oakdale (all West).

Entrance Fees   (may change)

- Vehicle (valid for 7 days) $20
- Individual (e.g. in a bus) $10
- Over 62 (US resident) $10
- Blind or disabled (US resident)   Free
- 1-Year Pass to Yosemite $40
- 1 Year Pass to All National Parks $50

Note: Due to the Jan 1997 floods and congressional legislation, the information above is subject to change.

Fun Things To Do In (or around) Yosemite Valley

Year Round

- Take a **Photography Class**. Experienced photographers give you tips in Awhahnee or Cook Meadow. Sign up at the Ansel Adams Gallery, Ahwahnee Hotel or Yosemite Lodge. The two-hour classes start around 8:30 or 9am.
- Fed up of photography? Take a free **Painting Class** instead and *create* the picture you want. Sign up at the Art Activity Center.
- Tour the **Ansel Adams Gallery**. An inspiring collection of books and prints will soon get you off that painting kick and back to the real action.
- Go **Hiking**. There are over 800 miles of trails so it'll take you a while to do them all. Favorite routes are up Yosemite Falls (start behind Sunnyside Walk-In) and up Vernal/Nevada/Half Dome.
- **Rent A Bike**. It's easier than hiking. There are 8 miles of rideways along the flat valley floor, and Mirror Lake makes a good destination. Bikes cost $16 a day from Curry Village.
- Go **Horseback Riding**. It's more elitist than biking. Trot around the valley or up to Vernal Fall. ☎209-372-8348.
- Forget traveling altogether and watch a Yosemite-themed play at the **Theater**.

Summer Only

- Go **Rafting.** Terrific fun, especially for children. Rent rafts and paddles at Curry Village ($12.50). You can spend the day floating down the cool river (take pictures with a disposable waterproof camera), then catch the free shuttle bus back.
- Go **Fishing**. A license is required but you might catch a raft.
- If rafting or fishing don't give you a rush, learn to **Rock Climb** at Yosemite Mountaineering School. Call 209-372-8435 for details or ask at the School's store at Curry Village. In the Spring & Autumn classes are held in Yosemite Valley; Summer in Tuolumne Meadows. You'll be climbing the 3,593' sheer face of El Capitan in no time (not!).

- Watch **the rock climbers** from the base of El Capitan or from Taft Point.
- Watch the **Hang Gliders** that leap from Glacier Point. This requires getting up early on weekend mornings as they usually finish by 8am.
- Step back in time at the **Pioneer History Center** where school groups dress in costume and character. Tours start at the Covered Bridge in Wawona.

Summer Evenings

- Take the sunset **Kodak Photo Tour** to Glacier Point and get some practical tips.
- The more romantic can take a two-hour **Moonlit Tour** of the valley.
- Astronomy buffs can watch the night sky from the **Observatory** on Glacier Point. Now there's a good place for an ultra-long exposure shot.
- There are other **Evening Programs** on natural history, outdoor adventure, storytelling, and music. at the LeConte Memorial, Shuttle stop #12.
- Watch the **Ansel Adams Photographer** film (about one hour long) at the Visitor Center's West Auditorium.

Winter Only

A certain 'snow' theme pervades these excursions:

- Take a ranger led **Snowshoe Tour**.
- **Ski Cross-country** to Glacier Point and see what Half Dome looks like in the snow. Bring your own gear and start at the junction of Route 41 and Glacier Point Road.
- Go **Downhill Skiing** at Badger Pass.
- Go **Ice Skating** at the delightful outdoor rink in Curry Village.
- Load up on film and gloves and **photograph** El Capitan from Gates of the Valley and the ice cones on Yosemite Falls.

Book Ahead

- Take a **Field Seminar**. 1-7 day outdoor classes in botany, geology, photography, art, or poetry. ☎209-379-2321.

Yosemite Valley is beautiful all year, though it's beauty changes with the seasons. The marginally best time to visit is late Spring, particularly mid-May, when the waterfalls are at their fullest. In Winter and Spring, the roads across the Sierras (120/Tioga Pass, 108, 4) are closed so don't plan on going farther east. I-80 and 50 usually stay open.

The climate is always mild. For the current weather , call 209-372-0200.

Spring

The melting snowpack floods the waterfalls producing awe-inspiring power. Concentrate on the dramatic waterfalls, particularly Yosemite Falls and Bridalveil Fall which significantly decrease in the Summer. Some transitory Falls appear, such as the whispy Horsetail Fall (east side of El Capitan) and Ribbon Fall (west side of El Capitan).

The Mist Trail is like walking through a heavy rainfall so carry a rain-proof jacket and wrap your camera in a plastic zip-lock bag. The Merced River swells and in some places overflows creating small reflecting lakes. Apple trees and dogwood trees blossom with large white flowers. The higher elevations (Glacier Point, Taft Point, top of Half Dome) are closed so you can't get those shots.

Summer

Unfortunately Yosemite Falls and, to a lesser extent, Bridalveil Fall, dry up by August as their granite watersheds don't hold the spring runoff. Instead, concentrate on Vernal and Nevada Falls which remain active.

The higher elevations open around Memorial Day so explore Glacier Point, Taft Point, or take a strenuous all-day hike to the top of Half Dome. Tioga Pass is now open also so you can drive east to the delightful Tuolumne Meadows, and maybe to Bodie Ghost Town and Mono Lake.

Over 20,000 people visit on Summer weekends and the rangers may delay traffic after 10am. This is not a pleasant result after a four-hour drive, so plan on arriving early. Temperatures can exceed 100°F so keep your film in the ice chest, wrapped in zip-lock bags.

Autumn

The crowds disappear by mid-September. The fall foliage is fabulous so concentrate on views of Half Dome from the meadows near the Ahwahnee Hotel & Curry Village, Sentinel Bridge, the Chapel, and Valley View. The Merced River is now placid and offers a great reflection of Half Dome from Sentinel Bridge.

Temperature

Min/Max in °F

Jan	26-49
Feb	28-55
Mar	31-59
Apr	35-65
May	42-73
June	48-82
July	54-90
Aug	53-90
Sept	47-87
Oct	39-74
Nov	31-58
Dec	26-48

Winter

Winter is the favorite season for many photographers. Thick snow lines the banks of the Merced River, creating idyllic shots of El Capitan from Valley View, and Half Dome from Mirror Lake. Cones of snow form at the base of waterfalls, particularly Upper Yosemite Falls, as the water freezes on it's descent. Low clouds settle in the valley, adding a primeval mood to your shots. Sunset from Tunnel View before or after a storm can be truly spectacular.

The temperature is down in the mid-20s to mid-50s, but the valley seldom sees severe weather. Winter snow rarely accumulates more than two feet deep. Tire chains may be required between Nov-April and the best access is via Mariposa on Rt. 140. Tioga and Glacier Point Roads are closed although you can still reach Glacier Point on cross country skis. From November to March a large outdoor ice rink opens at Curry Village and there's skiing at Badger Pass.

Best Time Of Day

The light moves magically over the west-facing valley. To get the best photographs, visit the sights at the following times:

8:30 ish: Take a photography class

Morning: Yosemite Fall, Ahwahnee Hotel, Mirror Lake, Taft Point.

Noon: Tunnel View.

Afternoon: Vernal Fall, Nevada Fall, Glacier Point, and Half Dome from Sentinel Bridge.

Late Afternoon: Mist Trail, Bridalveil Fall, Valley View, Mariposa Grove.

Sunset: Tunnel View, Bridalveil Fall. Half Dome from Glacier Point or Sentinel Dome.

Sunrise & Sunset Times

	Sunrise (am)	Sunset (pm)
Jan	7:20	5:05
Feb	6:54	5:40
Mar	6:14	6:10
Apr	6:27	7:39
May	5:51	8:08
June	5:37	8:29
July	5:50	8:27
Aug	6:16	7:57
Sept	6:44	7:11
Oct	7:12	6:25
Nov	6:45	4:49
Dec	7:14	4:42

* Times are for the middle (15th) of each month. For example, sunset for July 31 or Aug 1 would be about 8:15pm (between 8:27 & 7:57). For exact times, ask at the Visitor's Center.

Time Zone

Yosemite National Park, along with the western US, is in Pacific Standard Time (GMT-8 hours). Daylight Savings Time adds one hour (GMT-7 hours) and lasts from the first weekend in April to the last weekend in October.

Tunnel View is located at Longitude: 120°41' W; Latitude: 38°43' N.

Days with a Full Moon

	1997	1998	1999	2000
Jan	23	12	1 & 31	20
Feb	22	11	-	19
Mar	23	12	2 & 31	19
Apr	22	11	30	18
May	22	11	30	18
June	20	9	28	16
July	19	9	28	16
Aug	18	7	26	15
Sept	16	6	25	13
Oct	15	5	24	13
Nov	14	4	23	11
Dec	13	3	22	11

* Numbers represent the day of month when a full moon occurs.

How To Predict A Rainbow

Rainbows are scientific phenomena which can be accurately predicted. A rainbow occurs when sunlight passes through a fine spray, such as at the base of a waterfall, and is refracted into it's component colors - red through violet.

You can see rainbows at the base of Vernal Fall and Bridalveil Fall in the late afternoon, when you're standing directly between the fall and the sun. A circular halo will form with a 42° radius, around a point exactly opposite the sun.

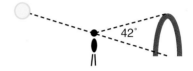

Bridalveil Fall in the afternoon is the best place to catch a rainbow.

Rain or Shine?

	Jan	April	July	October
Chances of a Sunny Day	39%	70%	97%	81%
Chances of Rain	26%	20%	3%	6%

Photo Walks

An excellent feature of the park is the availability of informative Photo Walks. These walks are offered daily in the summer, less frequently in other seasons, and are all staffed by experienced professional photographers. They are an enjoyable way to meet people of a similar interest, and to get ideas and tips to use during your visit. The Walks last about two hours and are all highly recommended.

The **Morning Lights Photo Walk** (free) leaves 8:30am from the Ahwahnee Hotel or Yosemite Lodge. Sign up at the appropriate hotel tour desk. The **Ansel Adams Camera Walk** (free) meets at 9am at the Gallery porch. Sign up at the Gallery, by the equipment counter. The **Kodak Sunset Tour** ($7, summer only) leaves the Visitor's Center main parking area at 5pm and includes a roundtrip ride to Glacier Point. Sign up at the Tour booth, behind the Village Store. Check the *Yosemite Guide* (free as you enter the park) for actual dates.

Photography central in Yosemite is the **Ansel Adam's Gallery**. You could spend a morning here browsing the beautiful images of it's namesake artist, believing that Yosemite is not just a park but an entire exotic world. It's only a matter of time before a strange force overcomes you and you dash outside, camera in hand, in search of the next *"Clearing, Winter Storm"*.

Besides an excellent selection of Adams' prints and books, the Gallery sells an eclectic range of artistic photography books. Check out Galen Rowell's books with the Sierra Club. A small equipment department offers film (including high-end slide and medium format film), filters, and cleaning accessories. Cameras can be rented by the day, which is handy when, like me, your camera breaks on the first day. An organized person would stock up with film and equipment before leaving home, but the Gallery is a welcome haven for those of us who aren't so well blessed.

Open 9-5pm, ☎209-372-4413. There is a sister store at the Inn at Spanish Bay, on the Monterey Peninsula.

The **Village Store** also has a good selection of film, picture books, disposable cameras, and polarizer filters.

Annette Walklet gives advice to photographers on the Morning Lights Photo Walk.

Photo Tours

Several companies offer 1-7 day tours:

Yosemite Field Seminars	209-379-2321
Sierra Photo Workshops	916-974-7200
Workshops in the West	512-295-3348
Dramatic Light Nature	800-207-4686

"The [35mm] camera is for life and for people, the swift and intense moments of life." Ansel Adams

1 Hold It Steady

A problem with many photographs is that they're blurry. Avoid 'camera shake' by holding the camera steady. Use both hands, resting your elbows on your chest, or use a wall for support. Relax: don't tense up. You're a marksman/woman holding a gun and it must be steady to shoot.

2 Put The Sun Behind You

A photograph is all about light so always think of how the light is striking your subject. The best bet is to move around so that the sun is behind you and to one side. This front lighting brings out color and shades, and the slight angle (side lighting) produces some shadow to indicate texture and form.

3 Get Closer

The best shots are simple so move closer and remove any clutter from the picture. If you look at most 'people' shots they don't show the whole body so you don't need to either. Move close, fill the frame with just the face, or even overflow it. Give your shot some impact. Use a zoom to crop the image tighter.

4 Choose A Format

Which way you hold the camera affects what is emphasized in your shot. For tall things (Redwoods, Half Dome) a vertical format emphasize height. Use a horizontal format to show the dramatic sweep of the mountains.

5 Include People

Photographs solely of landscape and rocks are enjoyable to take but often dull to look at. Include some of your friends, companions, family, or even people passing by, to add human interest. If there's no one around, include yourself with the self-timer.

Have you ever got your photos back only to discover that something that looked awe-inspiring at the time looks dull on paper? This is because your eye needs some reference point to judge scale. Add a person, car, or something of known size to indicate the magnitude of the scenery.

6 Consider Variety

You may take the greatest shots but if they're all the same type or style, they may be dull to look at. Spice up your collection by adding variety. Include landscapes and people shots, close ups and wide angles, good weather and bad weather. Take personal shots that remember the 'being there' - friends that you meet, your hotel/campsite, transportation, street or hiking signposts.

7 Add Depth

Depth is an important quality of good photographs. We want the viewer to think that they're not looking at a flat picture, but through a window, into a three-dimensional world. Add pointers to assist the eye. If your subject is a distant mountain, add a person or a tree in the foreground. A wide angle lens can exaggerate this perspective.

8 Use Proportion

The beauty of an image is often in it's proportions. A popular technique with artists is called the *rule of thirds*. Imagine the frame divided into thirds, both horizontally and vertically, like a Tic-Tac-Toe board. Now place your subject on one of the lines or intersections.

Always centering your subject can get dull. Use the Rule of Thirds to add variety and interest.

9 Search For Details

It's always tempting to use a wide angle lens and 'get everything in'. However, this can be too much and you may loose the impact. Instead, zoom in with a longer lens and find some representative detail. A shot of an entire Sequoia Tree just looks like a tree. But a shot of just the wide base, with a person for scale, is more powerful.

10 Position The Horizon

Where you place the horizon in your shot affects what is emphasized. To show the land, use a high horizon. To show the sky, use a low horizon. Be creative.

1 Use a Narrow Tonal Range

Photographic film can't handle a wide tonal range. When you photograph very bright things and very dark things together (sunlight in water and shadows in trees) the film will loose all the detail and you'll end up with stark overexposed white and total underexposed black. Instead, look for mid-tones with little difference between the brightest and darkest highlights. Flowers and trees for example are often best photographed on overcast, drizzly days.

Your eye can handle a difference in brightness (a 'dynamic range') of about 2,000:1 (11 camera 'stops'). Print film is limited to no more than 64:1 (5 stops) and slide film is even worse, at 8:1 (3 stops). Ansel Adams' 'Zone System' divided light levels into 11 'zones' and advised using a narrow zone (or tonal) range.

2 Work The Subject, Baby!

As film directors say, film is cheap (although it's not always their money!). Work the subject and take different shots from different angles. The more you look, the more likely you are to get a good one. Don't be afraid to take five shots and throw four away. Find different, unusual viewpoint. Shoot from high and from low. It's often said that the only difference between a professional photographer and an amateur photographer is that the professional throws more shots away. National Geographic magazine uses only 1 out of every 1,000 shots taken. (8/95 issue)

3 Hyperfocal

A popular 'pro' technique is capture great depth by combining a close foreground and deep background. Use a wide angle lens (20-28mm), get a few inches from the foreground (often flowers), put the horizon high in the frame. Using a small aperture (f22) keeps everything in focus ('hyperfocal'). Use a hyperfocal chart to correspond distance with aperture, or just use the smallest (highest f-number) possible.

4 Expose For Highlights

When a scene has a mixture of very bright and very dark areas the light meter in

"Emphasis on technique is justified only so far as it will simplify and clarify the statement of the photographer's concept." Ansel Adams

How To Get Deep Colors

1. Use a polarizer filter
2. Shoot in the late afternoon
3. Use 'saturated' slide film
4. Use a narrow tonal range
5. Keep your lenses clean
6. Underexpose slightly
   (for slide film - overexpose print film)

your camera will have difficulty finding the right exposure. In such high-contrast shots, try to expose for the highlights. To do this, walk up to, zoom in to, or spot meter on the most important bright area (a face, sky, detail) and half-depress the shutter release button to hold the exposure (exposure lock). Then recompose and take the shot. To be on the safe side, take several 'bracketed' shots.

5 Underexpose for Deeper Colors *SLR only*

On slide film, a slightly underexposed image (on print film a slightly underexposed image) can give deeper, more saturated colors . The deeper color also makes the subject appear heavier. On a manual SLR camera, select the next shutter speed up (1/250 when 1/125 is recommended by the meter). On automatic camera, set the exposure compensation dial to -1/2 or -1. Similarly you can underexpose for paler, lighter images.

The effect is dependent upon your camera and film so try some test runs to find the best combination. On my camera (a Minolta X-700 with Fuji Velvia film) the recommended exposure worked best and underexposure just lost detail.

6 Bracketing *SLR only*

Always expose for the most important highlight. When in doubt about the correct exposure, take several 'bracketed' shots. You 'bracket' around a shot by taking one regular shot, then a second shot slightly darker (-1 stop) and a third shot slightly lighter (+1 stop). Some cameras offer this as an automatic feature.

"Chance favors the prepared mind."
Louis Pasteur

1 Camera

It helps. Most of the photographs in this book can be taken with the cheapest of cameras. As the adage goes, it's not what you've got, but what you do with it. At heart, a camera is a box with a hole in it, letting a precise amount of light fall on the film, so a cheap 'box' doesn't necessarily mean poor pictures.

The main advantage of a more expensive camera is the ability to use different lenses. Basic 'compact' or 'point-and-shoot' cameras have a lens 'size' of around 35mm. This means that your photograph will include everything within a certain angle. A higher-end 'compact' camera may have a second lens size, say 70mm, and may allow you to 'zoom' between the two (say 35-70). With a longer 'telephoto' lens, you can zoom 'tighter' into a shot.

An 'SLR' (Single-Lens Reflex) camera allows you to disconnect the lens and use different lenses. Some photographers may carry up to ten lenses, and two camera 'bodies'. This is a more cumbersome approach but it allows greater flexibility in composing your shot. More on this later.

2 Polarizer Filter

The one accessory that will make the greatest improvement to your photographs is a 'polarizer' filter. Fortunately it's relatively cheap (around $15) and you can use it on any type of camera, even a compact camera. They are available at the Village Store and the Ansel Adams Gallery.

A polarizer filter maintains, or even adds, significant color to your shots, particularly deep blue skies. Without one, your shots may look washed out.

Normal light contains a lot of reflected light, or 'glare', which your eyes adjust for but your camera doesn't. A polarizer is like a very fine venetian blind and will filter out this glare. By rotating the filter from 0-90° it will remove a varying amount of glare, leaving deeper greens and blues. It is most effective when the sun is to one side of you (rather than behind or in front).

Most filters are designed to screw on to an SLR lens, so choose the diameter of your lens (e.g. 49mm or 55mm). With a compact camera, rotate the filter to the best orientation, then hold it over the camera lens and exposure elements. The Village Store sells a filter holder for compact cameras.

3 Film

Unless you need something specific, choose a well known print film, such as Kodak Gold Plus (the most popular in the US), Kodak Royal Gold (their premium print film), Fuji Super G Plus, or Fuji Reala (premium film). Print film ('color negative') is the best for prints and most enlargements - you're most likely purpose - and represents 90% of the film sold worldwide.

Slide film is preferred only for high end work (such as printing in magazines, entering in competitions, etc.), as the film holds deeper colors (it's more 'saturated'). All the shots in this book for example were taken on Fuji Velvia (ISO 50) film, famous for it's rich blacks, deep blues and vibrant greens. Kodak Ektachrome Elite and E100S is also popular, and produces more natural, less saturated images. But slide film is much more picky about exposure (less 'latitude') than the more forgiving print film, and, unless you're doing four-color book/poster/magazine printing, doesn't print as well.

The 'speed' of a film (100, 200, 400, etc) represents how quickly the film reacts to light. 200 is the most popular. If you're pictures come out blurry (you're prone to camera shake), use a 'faster' film such as 400 or 800. Most disposable cameras contain 800 or 1000 film for this reason. If you're looking for quality (entering a competition or enlarging photos), use 100 or 50 as the 'grain' or resolution is finer (although you won't notice it on a normal 4"x6"). Generally 'slow' film (100) is suggested for bright days, and 'fast' film (400, 800) for overcast, dim days.

Other film formats exist. 35mm (the image size is 36mm x 24mm) is the most popular and what your camera probably uses. The newer APS format (24mm x 16mm) prints almost as well and allows for much smaller, lighter cameras. Higher quality images are produced with larger film, such as 6cm x 6cm (2 1/4" square), 120mm or 220mm film. The cameras are much much larger and heavier, which is why professional photographers love the car parks at Tunnel View and Glacier Point.

4 Ice Chest

Normal print film is designed to be resilient so just make sure it's not left somewhere hot, like in a car trunk in 100° weather, or in sunlight. Professional film however is more sensitive and needs to be kept refrigerated. When traveling in the hot summer months, use an ice chest and buy a new bag of ice each day. Left unprotected in the trunk of a car for a few days, high-end film will shift red and wash out.

5 Lenses

A range of different lenses allows you a range of different shots. Most of the photographs in this book were taken with 28mm, 35mm, 50mm, 70mm, 135mm, 210mm and 300mm lenses. If you buy only one lens, let it be a 28-35mm zoom. A 20mm lens is the choice of many travel photographers.

6 UV/Skylight Filter

At higher elevations, such as Yosemite, UV light is more prevalent and will wash out your shot. Use a UV filter (about $12) to cut through the haze, particularly at Glacier Point, Taft Point and the top of Half Dome. Such filters also provide protection, in case you drop the lens.

7 Split-Field Neutral Density Filter

Film (particularly slide film) is much more sensitive to contrast than our eyes (see 'Tips'). At Sentinel Bridge (looking at Half Dome) or Gates of the Valley, the sky may be much brighter than the trees, which will produce an overexposed, white sky, and underexposed, black trees. To compensate, use a 'split-field neutral density' filter which is gray in the top half (toning down the sky), and transparent in the bottom. The filter compresses the contrast (reduces the dynamic range) so that the film can more accurately capture the shot.

Other filters: Many photographers use a warming filter (81B or 81C) to mimic the golden color of a setting sun. This is a matter of personal preference (most of the images in this book did not use an 81 filter, preferring instead the 'natural' look). Similarly color filters emphasize particular colors (CC20G for example adds 20% green). The general rule is: *'don't use a filter unless it serves some purpose'.*

8 Tripod

Everybody hates them - heavy, clunky tripods - but they're a necessity for quality shots. Generally, if your lens is longer than the exposure (e.g. 210mm at 1/60s - 210 is greater than 60), you're going to see camera shake on the final image. If you can't get a faster shutter speed (1/250s or 1/500s), either use a smaller lens (50mm) or a tripod.

Unfortunately heavy tripods are better, as they're more sturdy. Consider buying a shoulder strap or bag for hiking. For most applications a lightweight model will suffice. You can always rest your camera on a horizontal wall, against a tree, or on your poor companion's shoulder. A cable release avoids moving your camera when you press the shutter, or use the self-timer feature.

9 Storage

Dirty lenses or filters produce low-contrast images and washed-out colors. Keep things clean with a lint-free cloth, special dust-free tissues, lens cleaning fluid, and a blower brush. A small screwdriver can tighten up any screws that come loose, particularly on long lenses which don't like the vibrations of traveling.

Keep everything in a well-padded bag. Adjustable compartments are useful. Waistbags give you ready access to a range of lenses. Shoulder bags are popular but carrying the weight on one side all day can get uncomfortable. Backpacks allow you to keep your hands free and maintain balance when walking and hiking. If you're considering entering shots for competitions, you'll need a notepad and pen to remember camera settings and subject details.

10 Extra Supplies

Always carry a few extra rolls of film - you don't want to run out just before a spectacular sunset. It means spending more at the store but you'll use the film sometime. Carry a second, smaller camera (compact or disposable) for those quick, capture-the-moment shots. Also bring a spare set of batteries. As Gary Larsen (almost) said, just when you find the Loch Ness Monster, Bigfoot, and Elvis, all sitting together, your batteries die.

ANSEL ADAMS

One cannot discuss photographing Yosemite without paying homage to the work of Ansel Adams. Most of the classic views of the valley were first popularized by his expertly crafted images. His black and white prints, rich in tones and details, capture moody and heroic landscapes and are almost grander than the scenery itself. Our views of Half Dome, Vernal Falls, or the vista from Tunnel View, are forever influenced by his work.

"The best of his pictures stir our memory of what it was like to be alone in an untouched world."   John Szarkowski

Over a 50-year career, Ansel Adams (1902-1984) became America's best-known photographer. His name became almost synonymous with *Yosemite*. He helped establish landscape photography as an artform and inspired many to take a camera and find the beauty in nature.

San Francisco

The Adams family emigrated from Northern Ireland in the 1700's. Lured by the riches of the Gold Rush, Ansel's grandfather, W.J. Adams, moved to California in 1849. He soon saw that the money was not in joining the miners but in supplying them and opened a grocery store in Sacramento. He was neighbors of the future railroad barons (Huntington, Hopkins, and Stanford, who also greatly promoted travel photography). After his store burned down twice, W.J. saw the value of timber and built a chain of sawmills and a fleet of ships - the prosperous Washington Mill Company - inherited by his youngest son, Ansel's father.

Ansel Edward Adams was born in San Francisco in 1902. He was raised in a wealthy household, in a mansion overlooking Baker Beach, just south of today's Golden Gate Bridge. The earthquake and fires of 1906 destroyed most of the city but left the Adams' house untouched, and gave Ansel a broken nose which remained crooked. But a greater disaster was befalling the family. In the space of ten years, three of the sawmills had burnt down and 27 of the ships had been lost at sea or to fire. With no insurance, the fortune was lost. Another business venture failed (undermined by friends) and Ansel's father spent the rest of his life trying to repay the debts.

Despite the financial difficulties, Ansel's father resolved that the freedoms he was now denied would be given to his only son. He encouraged Ansel's gift as a self-taught pianist, and allowed him to visit the 1915 Panama-Pacific Exposition almost every day for a year. It was at this world's fair that Ansel first studied photography as a serious fine art.

Yosemite

Ansel Adams fell in love with Yosemite through a description in a book. In 1916, at his insistence, the family spent their 4-week summer vacation camping in the park. During this trip, his parents bought Ansel his first camera - a Kodak #1 Box Brownie.

Adams was captivated by Yosemite's beauty and visited the park every year for the rest of his life. In 1919, he got a summer job in the park looking after the LeConte Lodge, the headquarters of the Sierra Club. He led hikes, met learned people, and became a keen mountaineer.

Despite Adams' growing interest in photography, he intended to become a concert pianist. During the summers in Yosemite, he used the piano at the studio of Harry Best, who sold paintings, books, and souvenirs. Adams met and fell in love with Best's daughter, Virginia and they were married in the park in 1929. On Harry's death in 1936, the Adams inherited the studio and moved completely from the Bay Area to Yosemite. Best's Studio is still owned by the Adams family and is now operated as the Ansel Adams Gallery.

"Ansel Adams created some of the most influential photographers ever made, contributing more than any other photographer to the public acceptance of the medium as a fine art."
Jonathan Spaulding, biographer

Fine Arts Photographer

In the early 1920's, most of Adams' income came from taking publicity shots for the Yosemite Park and Curry Co., but he sold his personal work at Harry Best's studio.

Most of Adams' artistic photographs at this time were not of landscapes but more fine art, deliberately banal subjects, such as a single flower or a doorknob. It was not until Adams reached his late thirties and early forties that he concentrated on the style more familiar to us.

His art soon began to get noticed, and he was asked to work on a fine arts book about Taos, New Mexico - an opportunity which changed the direction of his career.

In Taos, in 1929, Adams met and befriended painter Georgia O'Keefe, whose husband was Alfred Stieglitz, a powerful force in photographic art. Stieglitz ran the influential gallery, *An American Place*, where Adams later exhibited what some consider the height of his fine arts work.

The next year in Taos, Adams met photographer Paul Strand and was moved by his work. Adams then decided to devote himself not to the piano, but to the camera.

Adams' photographs of Taos were published in 1930. He insisted on hand-printing every page and only 108 books were made. The price was a then-exorbitant $75, but every copy was sold in two years.

At that time, the style for fine art photographs was to look like charcoal drawings, with blurry, soft-focus images. But, along with other Bay Area photographers such as Edward Weston and Imogen Cunningham, Adams argued for clear, pure images. In 1932, they formed 'Group f/64', after the smallest aperture setting on a camera (which produces the sharpest, most focused images). They met only a few times but the Group was a seminal influence, turning the tide away from pictorialist images towards simple, straight prints.

Heroic Landscapes

On October 31, 1941, Ansel Adams took what is often considered the best-known image in the art of photography. While driving past the little town of Hernandez, New Mexico, he saw the light of the setting sun on the adobe buildings and church and stopped to take *Moonrise, Hernandez, New Mexico*. The image is famous for its deep velvet black sky, an element which Adams added years later with a different exposure in the darkroom.

"Photography is a way of telling what you feel about what you see."
Ansel Adams

In 1944 Adams took the classic *Clearing Winter Storm*. He had photographed departing snow clouds as they swirled majestically around the sweeping gates of the Valley, but he had captured an epic, delicate portrait, showing the ideal of nature. Adams and other photographers had photographed this vista hundreds of times before, but it is this grand, haunting, glorious vision of unspoiled America that is the most famous.

Much of Ansel's talent was utilized in the darkroom where he would spend days printing one shot. He wrote several technical books and codified his 'Zone System'. Adams allocated one of eleven 'zones' to each potential tone in a photograph -- 0 for deepest black, 5 for middle gray, and 10 for pure white. Techniques were then given for compressing or expanding the tonal range through printing to achieve the desired, 'visualized' image.

Adams continued his commercial work, producing huge transparencies for the Eastman Kodak Company to advertise their new color film. These 18' x 60' images of happy vacationers in front of waterfalls became a popular feature at New York's Grand Central Station.

Environmentalist

Adams became an energetic missionary for the Sierra Club. He raised awareness of the country's fragile land and natural resource and lobbied Congress for the establishment of King's Canyon National Park. The newspapers called him *"America's most influential environmentalist."* In 1942, Adams brought attention to the plight of interned Japanese-Americans at Manzanar with his sensitive photographs.

In 1962, Ansel and Virginia Adams and their two children moved to Carmel. The demand for his prints became so high that he stopped taking orders in 1975, but spent the next three years custom printing the 3,000+ pictures already requested.

Adams remained a keen conservationist and educator, teaching at California schools and leading photography tours of Yosemite in his trademark Stetson hat and gray beard. He continued to love music and enjoyed entertaining friends at his home. Perhaps it is fitting then, that on April 22, 1984, the day Adams died, his good friend pianist Vladimir Ashkenazy, played a recital in his honor at the Adams house.

Today

On Sunday evenings, the Visitor Center shows a 1-hour documentary on the life, spirit, and artistry of Ansel Adams. The Ansel Adams Galleries in Yosemite and on the Monterey Peninsular display his work to millions of visitors each year.

"No temple made with hands can compare with Yosemite. Every rock in its walls seems to glow with life. Some lean back in majestic repose; others, absolutely sheer or nearly so for thousands of feet, advance beyond their companions in thoughtful attitudes, giving welcome to storms and calms alike, seemingly aware, yet heedless, of everything going on about them."
John Muir

LOCAL RESOURCES

Print Developing
   Village Store
   Various mall stores in major towns

Slide Developing
Mariposa   **Photo Express**
   7th & Hwy 140. ☎209-966-2003
Sacramento   **Carmellia Color**
   2010 Alhambra at T St.
   ☎916-454-3801
   CFG Photo Lab
   20th & H St. ☎800-464-6861
   Ferrari Color
   601 Bercut Drive ☎800-533-6333
   Superlab
   733 Arden ☎916-649-2133

B&W Developing
Mariposa   **Photo Express** (see above)
Sacramento   **Palmer's**   (also   does
PhotoCD)
   2313 C Street ☎800-735-1950

Equipment
Yosemite   **Ansel Adams Gallery**
   Village Store
Mariposa   **Photo Express** (see above)
Merced   **Kits Cameras**
   Merced Mall ☎209-383-9011
   Camera & Video Center
   13th & J St. ☎ 209-524-7361
Fresno   **Boot's Camera**
   5587 North Blackstone.
   ☎209-432-0446
Reno **Silver State Camera**
   538 South Virginia Street.
   ☎702-323-9018
Sacramento   **Action Camera**
   1000 Sunrise Ave, Roseville
   ☎916-786-2288
   Pardee's Cameras
   3335 El Camino Ave, nr Watt
   ☎916-483-3435
San Francisco **Adolph Gasser**
   81 2nd Street.
   ☎415-495-3852

Repairs
Mariposa   **Mariposa Photographic**
   Hwy 140 & 8th St. ☎209-966-5211
Merced   **Camerafix**
   3528 N G St. ☎209-726-5000
Sacramento   **California Precision Service**
   1714 28th Street (Q & R St.)
   ☎916-451-1330
   Yong's
   10075 Folsom Blvd/Routier
   ☎916-362-5441

Further Information:
Yosemite National Park *(for Road &*
Weather   Information, Lodging and
Campground
   Information, Ranger-Led Activities,
   Trails, Permits)   **209-372-0200**
         TTY 209-372-4726 or 0294
Reservations
   Camping/Lodging   800-436-7275
         Outside-US   619-452-8787
   TTY   209-255-8345
   Lodging   209-252-4848
   Tours & Hikers Bus   209-372-1240
   Wilderness Permits   209-372-0740
   Bike Rentals   209-372-1208
   Gray Line Buses   209-384-1315
   Mountaineering School:
   Summer:209-372-8435; Winter:-8444
Other Services:
   Emergency (Fire, Med., Police)   911
   Medical Clinic   209-372-4637
   Dental Clinic   209-372-4200
   Ansel Adams Gallery   209-372-4413
   Lost and Found   209-379-1002
   Visitors Center   209-372-0299
   Bookstore   209-372-2648
Public Information   209-372-0265
Press Information   209-372-0248 & 0529
Yosemite Association   209-379-2646
Yosemite Field Seminars   209-379-2321
Yosemite Institute   209-372-9300
Yos. Mountaineering Sch'l 209-372-8435
Friends of Yosemite   415-434-1782
California National Parks   415-556-6030

Further Reading:
   Yosemite Visitor's Kit - includes The
Complete Guidebook to Yosemite National
Park, The Yosemite Road Guide, and maps
$14.95 ☎209-379-2648.
   About Ansel Adams: Ansel Adams, An
Autobiography; Ansel Adams: A Biography;
Ansel Adams and the American Landscape.

Internet Addresses
   For a current jumplist to related web
sites, as well as weather, photographs, and
updates to this book, visit:
   http://www.photosecrets.com

ORDER FORM & FEEDBACK

You can:

- Add your name to our mailing list;
- Tell us how to improve this book;

or

- Send us a distinctive or fun shot to be included in the next edition[1];
- Order another book.

☞ Cut out the FREE reply card below, or e-mail to **feedback@photosecrets.com**

--

☞ Send in a stamped envelope to: PhotoSecrets 9582 Vista Tercera San Diego CA 92129

Order Form

Please send me: _____ copy/copies of *PhotoSecrets Yosemite* at $7.95 each;
_____ *PhotoSecrets San Francisco & No. California* at $16.95 each;
Add: ❑ 7.75% sales tax if shipping within CA ($0.62 for Yos; $1.32 for SF&NC)
Shipping[2]: ❑ US: $4 first book +$1 for each add'l; ❑ CAN: $5 first +$1 ea. add'l;
❑ Europe & Mexico: $6.95 per book; ❑ Pacific Rim & elsewhere: $8.95 per book
Please mail your check (payable to *Photo Tour Books, Inc.*) to the address above.

Feedback

Comments/Suggestions/Compliments/Changes:

1. **Where did you buy this book?**

2. **What city/area/country would you like our next book to be about?**

3. **What camera do you use?**   ❑ Compact;   ❑ SLR;   ❑ Other format

4. **If you would like to be informed of future books and improvements, please add your contact information here:**

Name:

E-mail Address:

Street:

City & Zip/Postcode:

Country:

[1] When submitting photos, include a stamped addressed return envelope if you want them returned. Not responsible for any loss or damage.
[2] For each pair (Yosemite + SF&NC) the second book ships for free.

☺

☝

✉ Send other correspondence to:
PhotoSecrets
9582 Vista Tercera
San Diego CA 92129

✂ ----------------------------------

From: PhotoSecrets Yosemite, v1.1

✂

**PhotoSecrets
9582 Vista Tercera
San Diego CA 92129**

Also Available:

Over 400 Pictures YOU Can Take

PhotoSecrets

SAN FRANCISCO
& Northern California

The Best Sights and How To Photograph Them

Includes:
- Big Sur
- Yosemite
- Redwoods
- Mono Lake
- Hearst Castle™
- The Gold Country
- The Wine Country
- Monterey & Carmel

Andrew Hudson
Foreword by Bob Krist

ISBN 0-9653087-1-5 • 352 full-color pages.

PhotoSecrets
Travel Guides for Travel Photography

Available at bookstores
and giftstores.

INDEX

Visit the web site:
http://www.photosecrets.com

Also available:
PhotoSecrets San Francisco and Northern California